This story is for my family.

The Little Brown Hen
Illustrations © 2015 - Casey Dilzer
(Water color and ink)
Printed in United States of America (USA)
Published by Great Books 4 Kids
(http://www.GreatBooks4Kids.org)
All rights reserved.

There once was a Little Brown Hen
who found some seeds in the barnyard.

"What shall I do with these seeds?"
thought the Little Brown Hen.

"I shall plant them,"
she thought to herself?

"But who will help me
plant my seeds."

"Will you help me plant these seeds?" she asked her friend, the Blue Dog.

"I will not," said the Blue Dog as he lazily watched the television from the farmer's couch.

"Will you help me plant my seeds?"
the Little Brown Hen asked the Purple Cat.

"Not now," said the Purple Cat as she primped and purred, looking at her reflection in the mirror.

"I am too busy for your nonsense."

Next, she asked the Green Donkey, "Will you help me plant my seeds?"

"No, I will not help you," said the Green Donkey as he kicked the barn fence.

"I am too busy waiting for Farmer Brown to bring me an apple."

"We could plant the seeds while we wait," said the Little Brown Hen.

"I prefer to wait alone," replied the Green Donkey.

The Little Brown Hen was disappointed that no one wanted to help. She had thought that it would be fun to work with the other farm animals to see what they could grow together.

Suddenly, the Little Brown Hen had an idea and was filled with joy and energy.

"I shall plant the seeds myself!"

So she did. She tended the seeds,
watered them, sang to them,
and weeded around them.

She knew her seeds would grow.

In no time, her seeds began to grow.

Everyone was surprised at how fast the seeds grew. It was like magic!

The Little Brown Hen was happy and she continued to take care of the seeds.

She even planted more seeds!

The Little Brown Hen was dedicated to her work and she enjoyed watching the trees grow.

The trees gave her shade to sit in, food to eat, and a beautiful view.

Bees and butterflies visited the trees to pollinate, and the Little Brown Hen was happy.

One day, the Purple Cat, the Blue Dog, and the Green Donkey came to ask the Little Brown Hen a question.

"Why don't you sit down?" asked the Green Donkey. "You are always tending to things."

"Because I enjoy life and do not wish to waste my time or talents," replied the Little Brown Hen.

"Why don't you watch television?" asked the Blue Dog.

"Because I prefer to create my own reality," replied the Little Brown Hen.

"Why don't you care about getting dirty and dusty?" asked the Purple Cat.

"I enjoy my work and I love the dirt, the sun, the water, and the trees. Doing this makes me happy and provides me with all that I need," replied the Little Brown Hen.

"Now I have a question for you," said the Little Brown Hen to the Blue Dog, the Purple Cat, and the Green Donkey.

"Rather than wasting your time and talents being lazy, playing pretend games, and primping while you wait for Farmer Brown to give you food, why not join me? We can create amazing things together," said the Little Brown Hen.

"Let's plant these seeds today and soon we will have enough to harvest. Let's work together and use our talents to bring us joy. We can create our own reality through our work and ideas," said the Little Brown Hen.

"Let's share our ideas with everyone and watch as they spread like wildfire!" said the Little Brown Hen.

About the Author

Leticia Colon de Mejias lives in Connecticut with her husband, children, and their dogs, Bio-diesel and Cuddles. Leticia's motivation for doing all she can to help the environment comes from her love of children and nature. She has authored and illustrated many children's books including: *"Butterfly Rhythm," "Hip Hop and the Wall," "Mrs. Busy Bee," "Pesky Plastic,"* and *"Over the Moon and Past the Stars."* She donates time and books to local schools and libraries. Leticia founded the Green Eco Warriors , a non-profit, after watching *"Kilowatt Ours* and *Message in the Waves."*

About the Illustrator

Casey Dilzer strives to be involved in projects geared toward motivating and influencing children to create. She has illustrated several books including: *"Over the Moon and Past the Stars," "Saturday,"* and *"Dinero Defeats the Phantom Draw."* She is a co-author for the *"Green Eco Warriors"* comic book series and is continuously creating educational tools for children.

Other Great Books 4 Kids

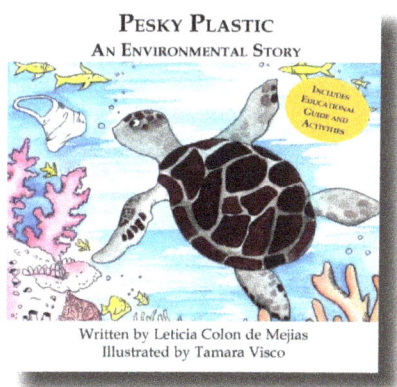

Pesky Plastic: An Environmental Story is a fun and educational book about plastic and its impact on our planet. Discover the dangers of "pesky plastic" in our oceans. Learn what you can do to help Sally, Allen, Pat and all the sea animals survive "pesky plastic." This ecology-centered story is a wonderful way to begin conversations with children about how each person's actions directly affect the environment. Aligned with Next Generation Science Standards.

Follow along as the Green Eco Warriors take on Mr. Corp and his cohorts the Medler, the Phantom Draw and many others. It's going to be a demanding battle for the Green Eco Warriors. If they can lay aside their individual troubles and make sacrifices for the betterment of the planet, then maybe they stand a chance.

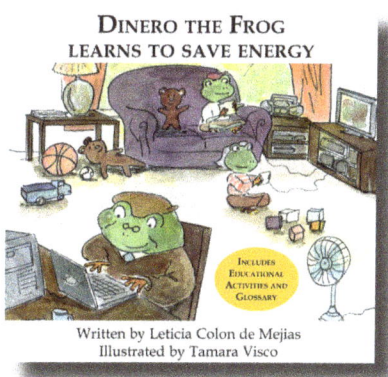

Dinero the Frog Learns to Save Energy is a fun and educational book about energy conservation. Poppi the Frog teaches Dinero about energy, where it comes from, how it is used, and what we can do to conserve energy and reduce pollution. Aligned with Next Generation Science Standards.